The Banjo Music of Tony Ellis

Original Tunes and Arrangements in Tablature and Notation

Music written and arranged by Tony Ellis
Banjo tablatures by Gil Benson and Gary Puckett
Standard notation by Gil Benson
Foreword by Stephen Wade

ISBN 1-57424-140-0
SAN 683-8022

All compositions in this book are copyright 1987, 1993, 1998, and 1999 Merrywang, Inc. and used with kind permission.

~ Foreword ~

Tony Ellis quietly took hold of his banjo. It was the first night of the 1983 National Folk Festival, held that year in Peninsula, Ohio. With the evening's concert winding down a few miles away, performers and staff began to return to their hotel. Participants from the event—African *griots* and East Indian musicians, Appalachian singers and Piedmont blues guitarists—informally gathered in this windowless, basement conference room, empty but for a stack of metal banquet chairs lined up against the wall and a table set with light refreshments. A *tamburitzan* band from Cleveland, still in costume from their performance, grabbed a few beers and tuned up to play, while a revered Cajun performer affectionately spoke of his travels overseas, his hands encircling his old violin. Soon, music making of all sorts filled the room and spilled into the neighboring hallways. In the midst of this joyful din, Tony showed me what he had in mind for the banjo workshop scheduled for the next day.

He drew his second string up to C, while lowering the bass down to C. He still wore his metal fingerpicks and played his Gibson-style resonator banjo—sure signs of his background in bluegrass—but his tuning pointed to an earlier musical era. Though Tony profoundly loves the phrasing of Scruggs-style banjo (after all, he had been a member of Bill Monroe's Blue Grass Boys from 1960 to 1962), he also loves old-time music for its tunefulness. He began to play a version of "Sally Anne" that he had learned from Tommy Jarrell, the masterful fiddler from Mt. Airy, North Carolina, Jarrell's nineteenth-century sound intersecting with Scruggs's landmark style. Tony was weaving together two great strands of Southern music.

In the days after the festival, Tony began writing more tunes in this mode. The first was "Peninsula," named after the festival site where he had just been. Then came "Father's Pride," a gossamer-delicate banjo waltz written for his son. My travels to Tony's home to sift through his new tunes became a seasonal fixture for us both, and we looked towards making a record. In 1987, that work resulted in *Dixie Banner*, a collection that featured Tony's banjo and fiddle compositions in a variety of settings. For the title piece, his banjo seemingly led a small-town parade suggested by a puffing tuba, while a Scottish atmosphere of tin whistles and bagpipe-like drones surrounded his playing of "My Sweet Highland Girl."

Other recordings followed. In 1993, he completed *Farewell My Home*, a set of twenty-three tunes. All but one, the closing hymn, were products of his own imagination. Throughout the record, Tony was joined by his son Bill on guitar, a combination that emphasized the graceful sway of the writing. The following year, Tony became part of "Masters of the Banjo," a bi-coastal tour of exceptional traditional players who represented the instrument's evolution. On the accompanying album, Tony played several pieces of his own, touching two sources of his inspiration, both Southern and Irish. In 1998, he completed *Quaker Girl*, which included his Civil War-era fretless banjo, taking his new works even further back in time and texture. *Sounds Like Bluegrass to Me*, released in 1999, allowed him to commemorate the repertoire of songs that he first became exposed to as a young musician in the 1950s. Instilled in all these records is a sense of remembrance. Through his music, Tony recalls persons he has known and places he has seen. Moods, from jubilant to elegiac, contemplative to buoyant, mark his playing. From the titles alone, one gets a sense of what he values and whom he cherishes.

For banjo players, the rewards of his music extend even further. Here is a gifted bluegrass musician who has harnessed that skill to create a new body of old-time works. By translating his music into tablature (which, by the way, is a language that Tony himself doesn't read), others are given a glimpse into the sinews of the three-finger style. Tony's choices, the logic of his fingering, reveal an understanding of the instrument and the dictates of a style he has known all his life. While his compositions adapt that technique to a new end, they also reveal its essential nature. They offer a window into a great tradition.

Many of these performances are represented in this book. Ohio music teacher Gary Puckett completed an initial series of tablatures. Kentucky fiddler and banjoist Gil Benson revised and developed these tablatures as well as writing some new tablatures and transcribing all of it into standard notation in a publishable format. With Tony at his side, Gil checked each of the forty-four original compositions along with the three arrangements of traditional songs that comprise this collection. As the work neared its final stages, Steve Martin graciously contributed his comments. Tony's advice on playing the tunes precedes each entry.

Twenty years have passed since the first of these tunes was written. Tony Ellis's music—chiming, romantic, touching, and playful—remains evergreen. With this book, it also becomes all the more accessible.

Stephen Wade
Washington, D.C.
Spring 2003

To my banjo playing friends!

For most of my sixty years I have always loved the sounds of the banjo, whether they be from my grandmother who played a folk/parlor style, or old-time mountain banjo—fretted or fretless—rag-time, jazz, and Irish tenor to, of course, the wonderful bluegrass banjo music of Earl Scruggs. The tunes in this book reflect many moods and forms for banjo music that bring together old tunings (used mostly by frailing style players) with two and three-finger picking techniques more akin to bluegrass styles. Some of these tunes have found their way into films and theatre where I have long felt a strong interest. Some tunes have a strong melody line, and some are tunes that project atmosphere and dimension in time.

I hope you enjoy the tunes in this book in the ever-growing world of the banjo!

Sincerely,

Tony Ellis
Braeburn Farm Bed and Breakfast
6768 Zane Trail Road, Circleville, Ohio 43113
www.tonyellisbanjo.com

For publishing information:
Merrywang, Inc.
c/o Melford Law Office
12 Brattle Circle, Cambridge, Massachusetts 02138-4625

Edited by Stephen Wade. Special thanks to Jean Murphy and Dwight Holmes for their assistance. Additional thanks to Ilene Waterstone of Steve Martin's office, Donald and Spencer Nitchie of *Banjo NewsLetter*, as well as Louise Adkins, Bill Ellis, Pete Kuykendall and *Bluegrass Unlimited*, Judy McCulloh, Larry Nager, Michaelle LaFond Wade, and Ron Middlebrook.

Contents

Barefoot Boys

"Barefoot Boys" is pretty simple to play, as are most of my tunes. I might point out
in playing the B part that the melody is led with the thumb, building rolls from that
point. This is a technique I learned from Earl Scruggs. On the recording the guitar was
capoed at the 5th fret to play out of a G position to give the tune a bluegrass flavor.

Form: AA BB AA B1B1 A1A1 BB AA

Composed by Tony Ellis

Tuning: gCGCD   Capo 1

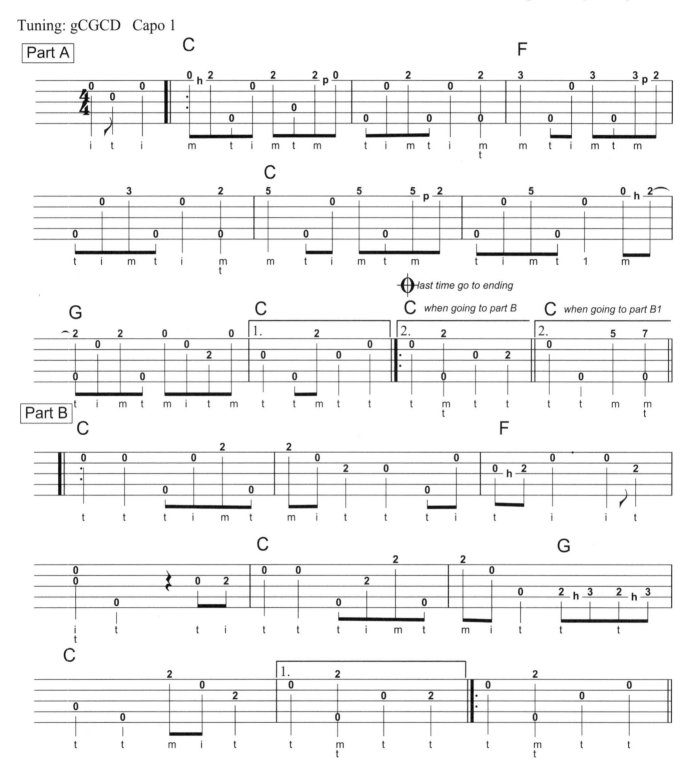

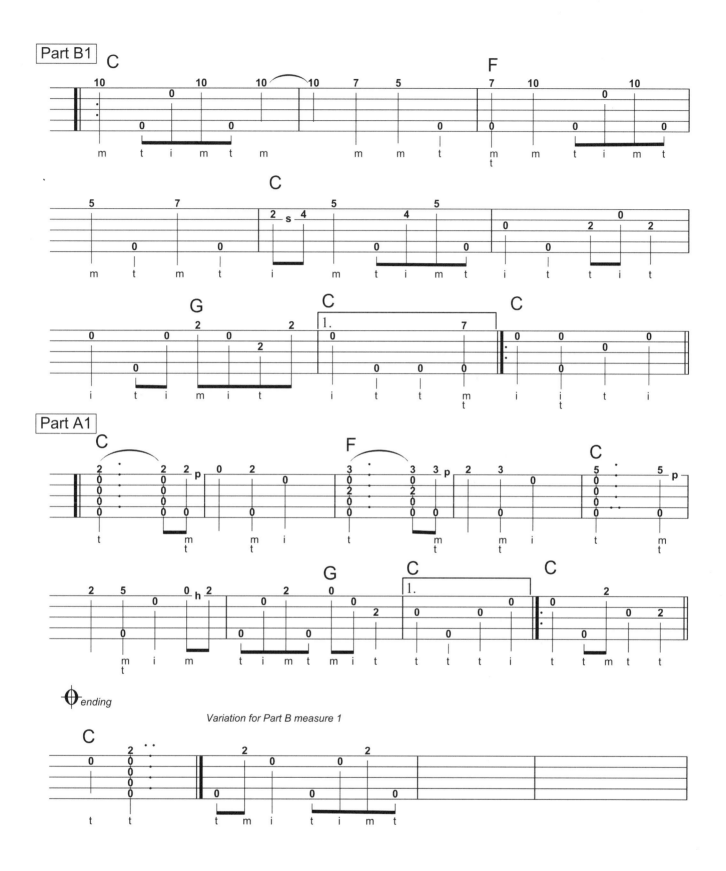

Barefoot Boys

Tony with tenor banjo, Lynchburg, Virginia, 1955.

Big Bad Red

On "Big Bad Red's" A part, 2nd and 6th measures, the hammer on/pinch on the 2nd string at the 3rd to 4th fret can be played on the 1st string at the 1st to 2nd fret, but the second string position gets your left hand closer to the next note. That is the better procedure. The pinch on the B part requires that the index finger and middle fingers play the 3rd and 2nd strings.

Form: A BB C A BB C DD

Composed by Tony Ellis

Tuning: gCGCD

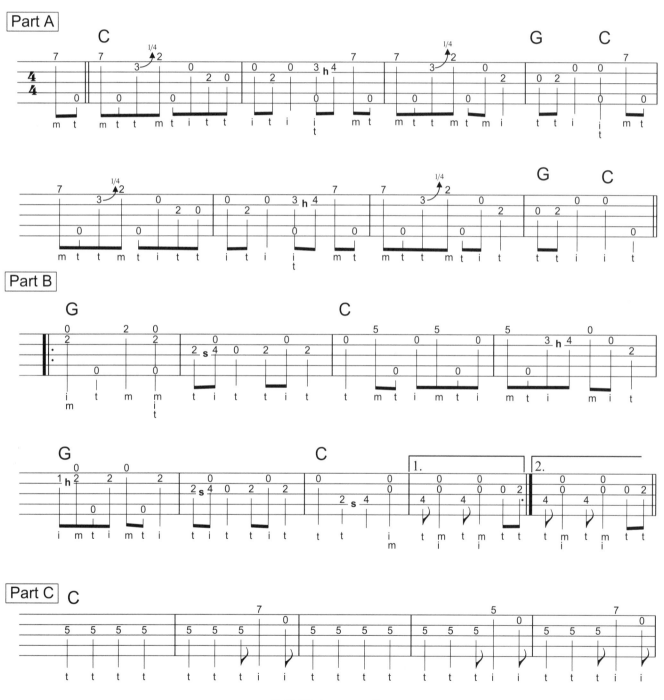

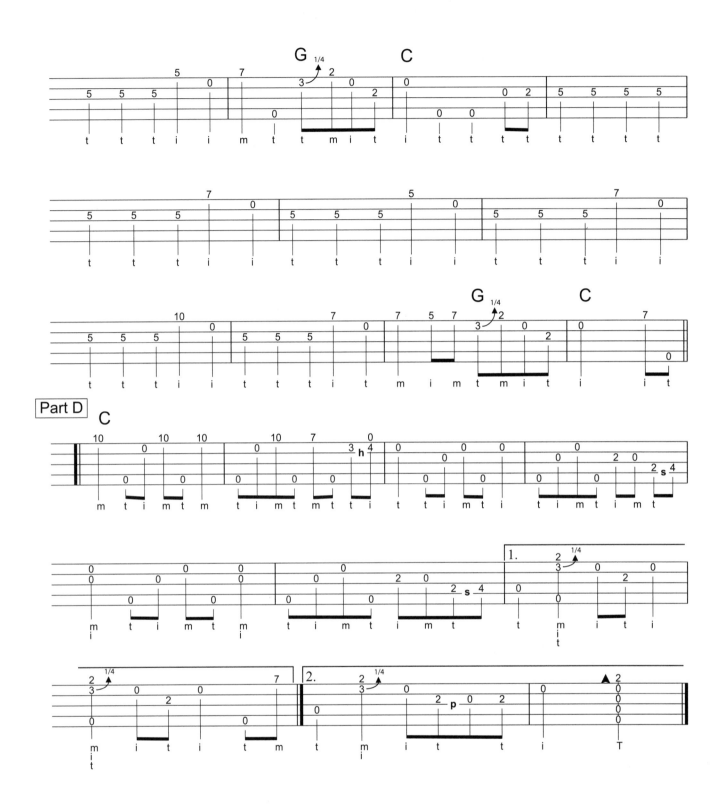

Big Bad Red

Cherry Blossom Waltz

"Cherry Blossom Waltz's" B1 part requires the right-hand index and middle fingers to play the 4th and 3rd strings entirely through this part. This tune has an easy melody to follow and is enhanced by some beautiful, simple guitar chords.

Form: AA BB AA B1B1 AA BB AA

Composed by Tony Ellis

Tuning: gCGCD capo 2

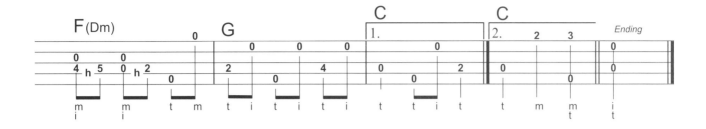

Cherry Blossom Waltz

Tony in Kuwahna City, Japan, 1992.

Come Thou Fount of Every Blessing

For the B part of "Come Thou Fount of Every Blessing," the right hand index and middle fingers play the 3rd and 2nd strings except for the F note (F chord) when the thumb plays the 3rd, index plays the 2nd, and middle plays the 1st. This tune is most effective when played at a slow, stately pace.

Form: A B A1 B1 A B

Tuning: gCGCD

Traditional, arranged by Tony Ellis

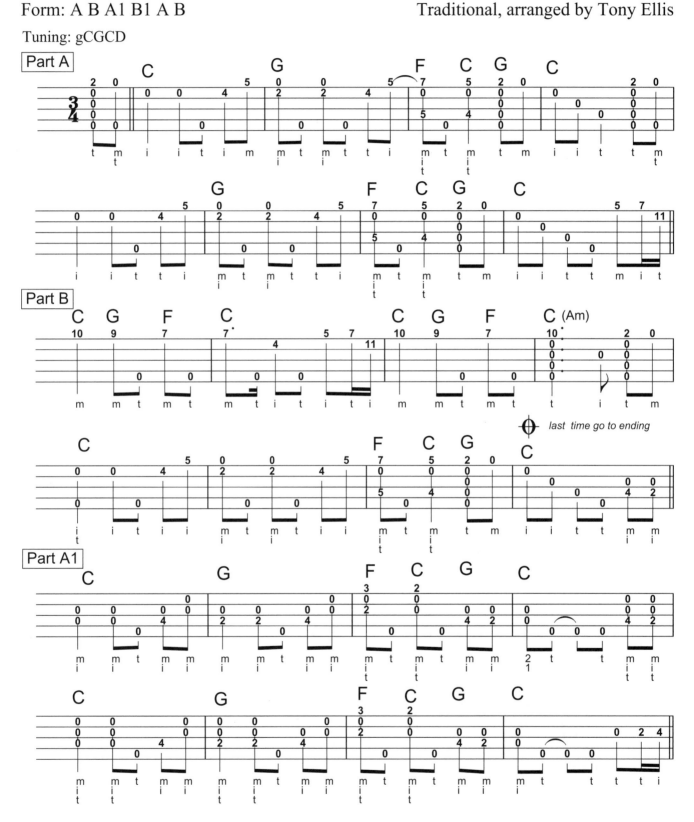

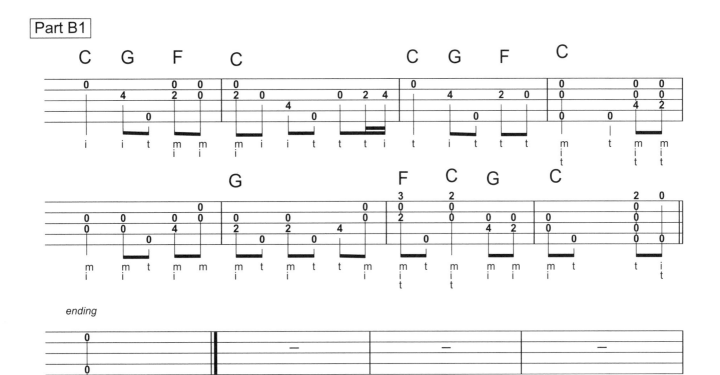

Come Thou Fount of Every Blessing

Courtner's Country Ham

"Courtner's Country Ham's" high note on the B1 part is pretty easy to get if you are sure to play the preceding note as an open 5th string (last note of measure 5) rather than playing a fretted note on the 1st string.

Form: AA BB AA B1B1 A1A1 B2B2

Composed by Tony Ellis

Tuning: gCGCD

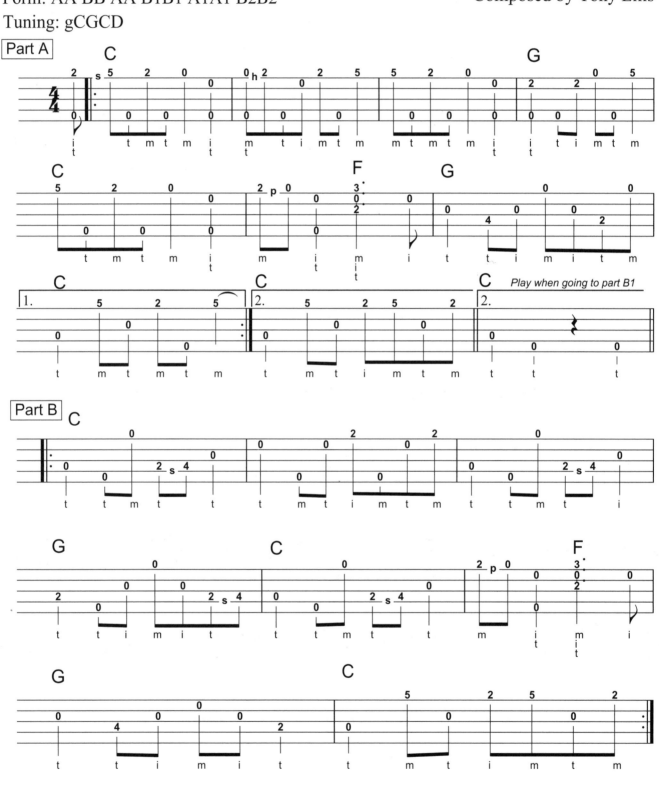

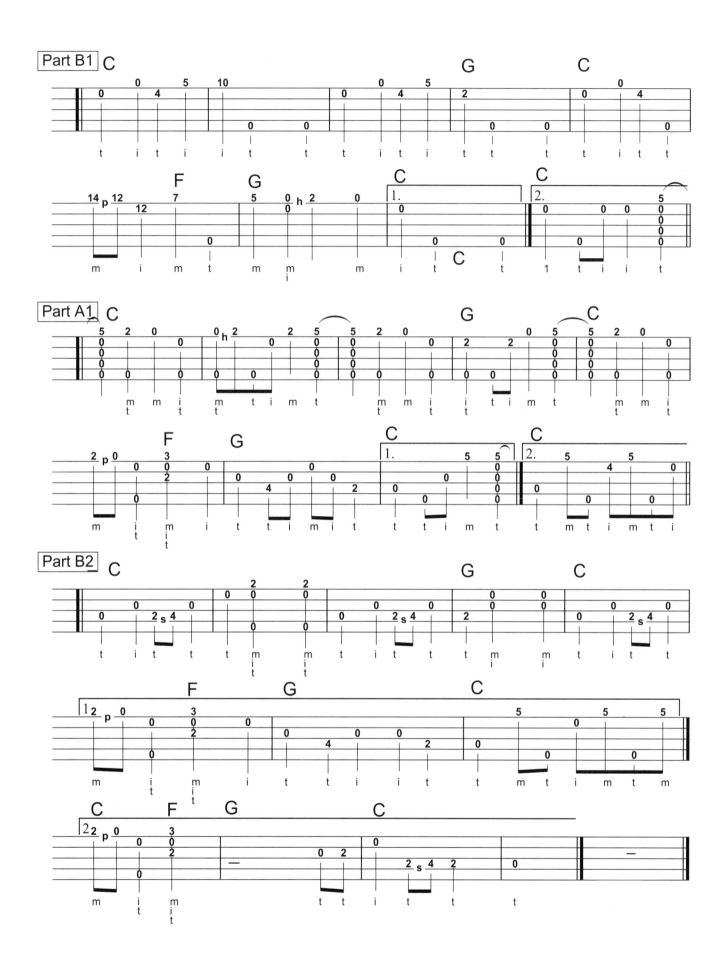

Courtner's Country Ham

Dawson George

"Dawson George" is pretty simple to play as long as the tempo is kept at a modest pace. The Cherokee music I recall hearing as a child had a modal sound, so I felt this to be the sound needed for this tune. Strength with feeling!

Form: AA BB AA BB AA BB AA

Composed by Tony Ellis

Tuning: gCGCD

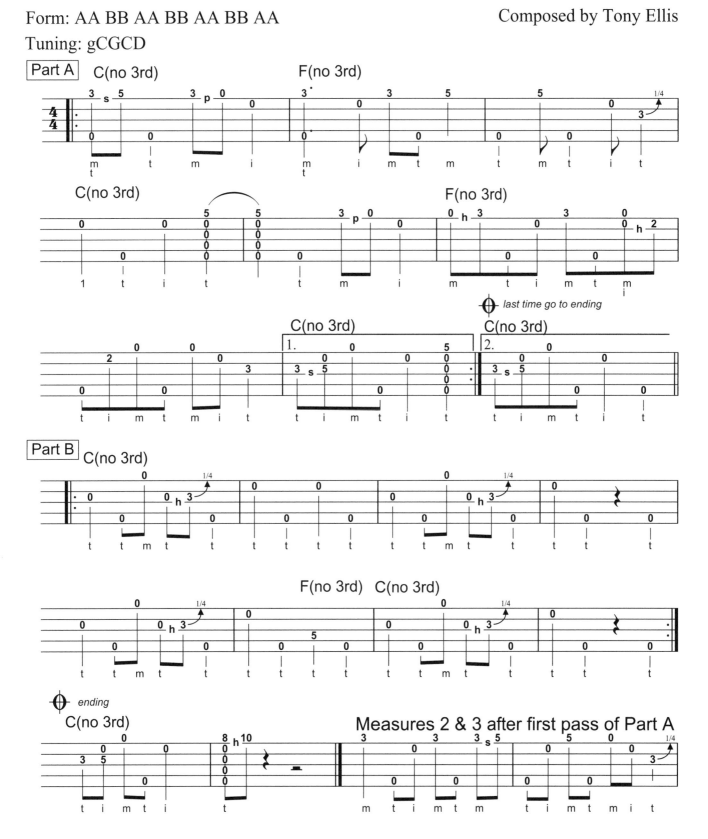

Dawson George

Tony, Bristol, Tennessee, late 1970s.

Dixie Banner

"Dixie Banner" is best when kept at a modest pace and not fast. The tune has a real "Americana" feel, on old tuning combined with the Scruggs' style right-hand and played as a march.

Form: AA BB A1A1 BB AA BB AA B1B1

Composed by Tony Ellis

Tuning: gCGCD

Dixie Banner

Doc Mongle's Blues

"Doc Mongle's Blues" almost sounds like a modal tuning at first, but it's standard. A sprightly instrumental employing the modal sounds and underlying polychord (F chord with unnoted G string). Doc was a wonderful banjo player as well as being a superb surgeon - just ask Ralph Stanley! This tune denotes the fun of banjo playing blended with a sense of urgency. Doc Mongle!

Form: AA BB AA BB A1A1 B1B1 AA BB

Composed by Tony Ellis

Tuning: gDGBD

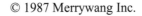

25

Doc Mongle's Blues

Dr. Bruce Mongle. Bristol, Tennessee, 1986.

Downtown 5th Street Rag

The pinch-hammer in "Downtown 5th Street Rag" on the 2nd string (3rd to 4th fret) is done on the 2nd string instead of the 1st to keep distance from the preceding note. This makes it easier to play. Almost a blues rag, somewhat related to the black blues of the early twentieth century.

Form: AA B AA B AA B

Composed by Tony Ellis

Tuning: gCGCD

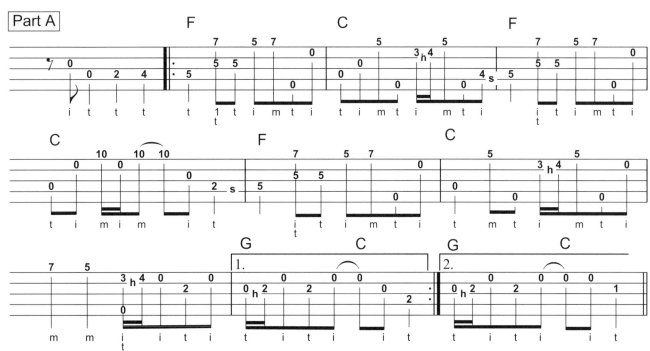

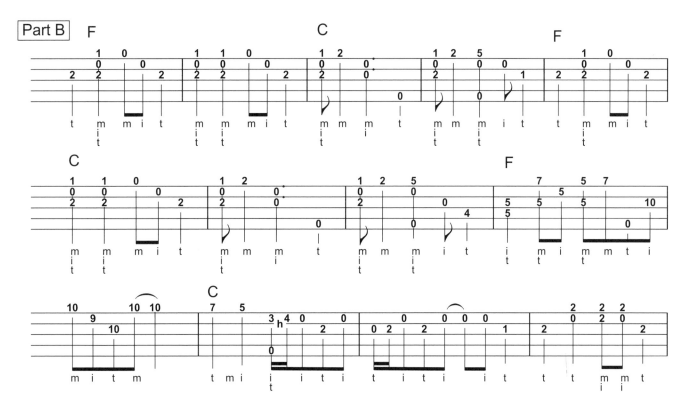

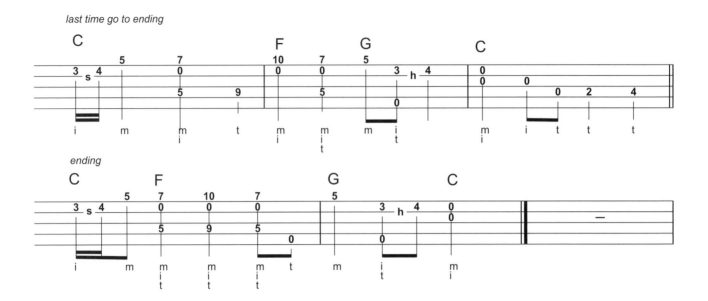

Downtown 5th Street Rag

Farewell My Home

By using this tuning in "Farewell My Home," with the low bass string tuned down to
F, the droning undercurrent reinforces the melody. The piece should be played gently,
but when its expression needs to be stronger, emphasize a particular note or passage.
By adding strength at such a point, you can bring further emotion to the tune.

Tuning: fFFCD

Composed by Tony Ellis

Farewell My Home

Father's Pride

"Father's Pride" is a slow waltz/lullaby played gently. This tune gives the voice of the banjo a chance to really speak in a way not often associated with the banjo with gentility and space.

Form: A BB A1 B1B1 A2A2 BB A

Composed by Tony Ellis

Tuning: gCGCD

Part B1

Part A2

ending

Play the following measure in place of Part B measure seven (7) the last time through:

Father's Pride

Bill and Tony Ellis, Circleville, Ohio, 1993

Going to the County Fair

"Going to the County Fair" is a real "Americana" tune that speaks to a long-past era that
embraced simplicity, humor, and appreciation for fundamentals. The underlying harmonies,
played on the open 2nd string as you move about on the neck, really can move you to
another time! It's easy enough to play but actually is better for a guitar accompanist if
the banjo capo is on the 2nd fret so the tune is played in D. Also, this tune is fun if
the guitar is in DADGAD tuning. A moderate pace is best.

Form: AA BB AA BB AA BB

Composed by Tony Ellis

Tuning: gCGCD

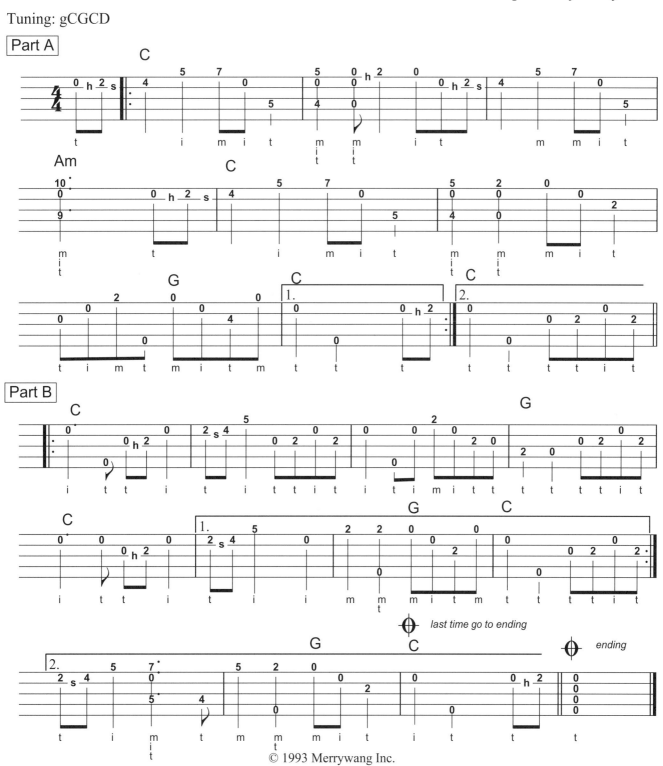

Going to the County Fair

last time go to ending

ending

Going to Town

The A part in "Going to Town" is played using three-finger technique, while the B part is mostly two-finger except when playing the bass string. The right-hand index and middle fingers move over one string to play the 3rd and 2nd strings as harmonies to the bass.

Form: AA BB AA BB AA BB AA

Composed by Tony Ellis

Tuning: gCGCD Capo 2

Going to Town

Tony, Lynchburg, Virginia, 1957.

Hand in Hand

"Hand in Hand" is a slow, gentle wedding air. Playing away from the bridge softens
the banjo for a sweeter tone. The Em fits very easily as does the next chord, F.

Form: AA BB AA BB AA BB

Composed by Tony Ellis

Tuning: gCGCD

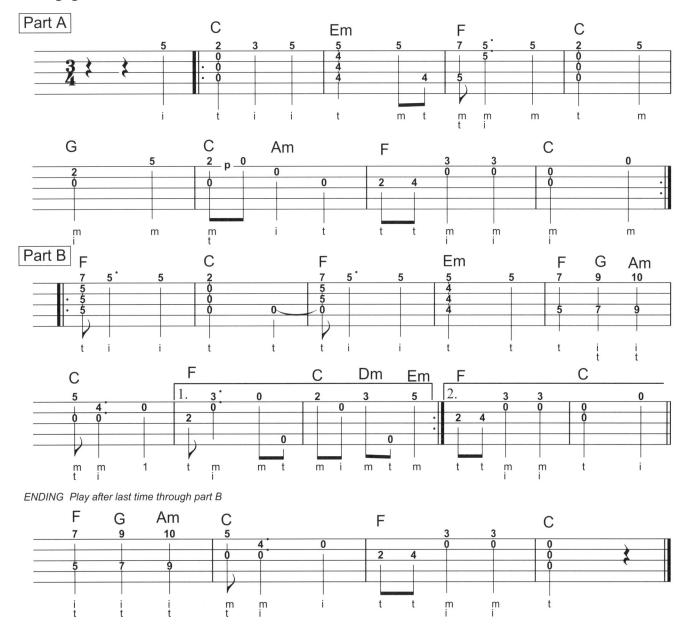

ENDING Play after last time through part B

Part B 2nd measure, the low C (4th string open) should ring until Em chord in measure 4.

Hand in Hand

Tony, Chillicothe, Ohio, 1984.

Hartford's Waltz

In 1992, at the Tennessee Banjo Institute, I was part of a banjo workshop with John Hartford.
I enjoyed watching him play and the movements he made. In "Hartford's Waltz," I
incorporated a bit of his hammer-on/pull-off and other techniques into this tune. John
was one of my heroes!

Form: AA BB A1A1 B1B1 A BB   Composed by Tony Ellis

Tuning: gDGBD

© 1993 Merrywang Inc.

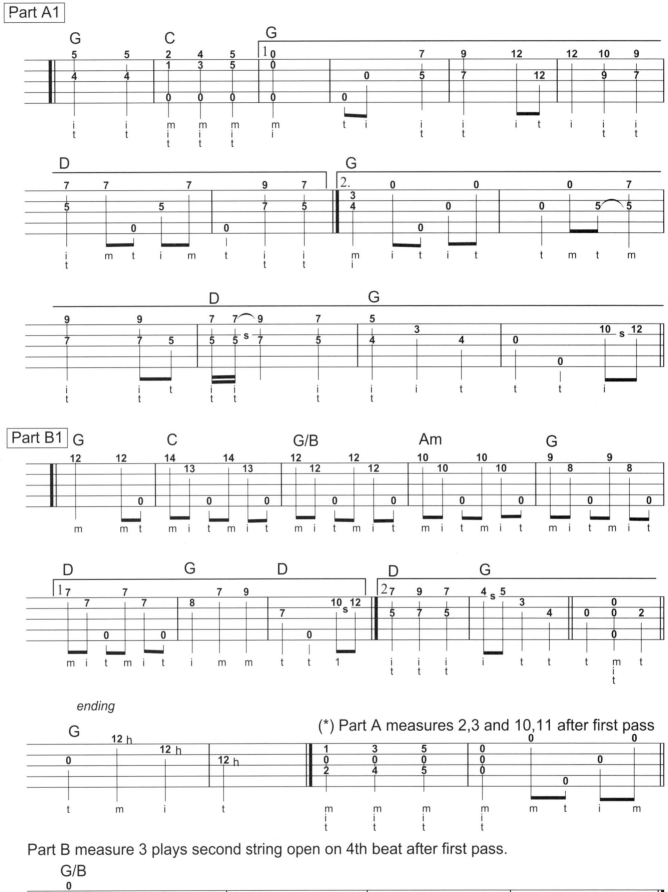

ending

Part B measure 3 plays second string open on 4th beat after first pass.

Hartford's Waltz

I Fell in the Fishing Hole

I love this F tuning!!!   It's a great banjo sound! There are some enjoyable rolls and spaces built into "I Fell in the Fishing Hole." The tune also gives a great opportunity to the guitar for fun things.

Form: A BB A BB A BB A BB

Composed by Tony Ellis

Tuning: fCFCD

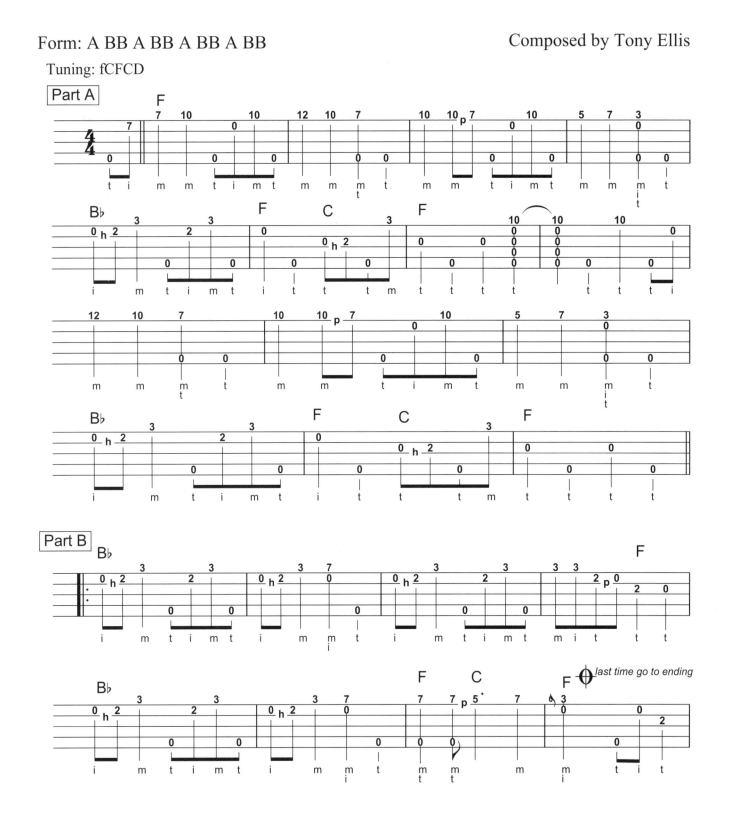

ending

NOTE: When returning to part A play
this instead of the 1st bar of A.

I Fell in the Fishing Hole

Kate, Bride of Matt

"Kate, Bride of Matt" is a musical conversation between a bride (high notes) and groom (low notes) which unites them through harmonies at the end of the tune. When playing the bass notes with the thumb, bring the right-hand index and middle fingers over one string to play the 3rd and 2nd strings. This creates nice harmonies and counterpoint and enforces the lower register (male part of the tune).

Tuning: gCGCD

Composed by Tony Ellis

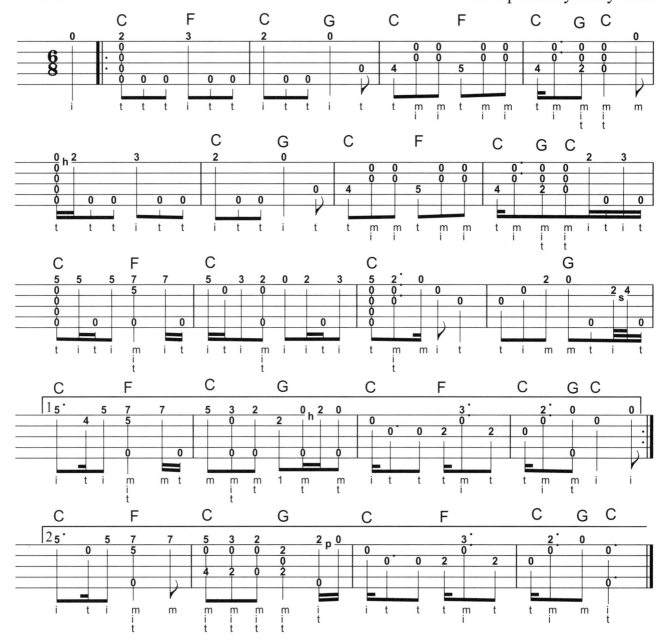

Kate, Bride of Matt

Tony, Charlottesville, Virginia, November 1999

Mama Juana

In "Mama Juana (Wana)," the B1 part is played in one position of the left hand:
the little finger on the 1st string at the 10th fret and the left index finger on the 2nd
string at the 7th fret. The ring finger notes the 2nd and 3rd string notes at the 9th fret.
The last note of that part is an open 2nd string. The guitar tuning is DADF#AD.

Form: AA BB AA B1B1 AA BB AA B1B1 AA

Composed by Tony Ellis

Tuning: gCGCD   Capo 2

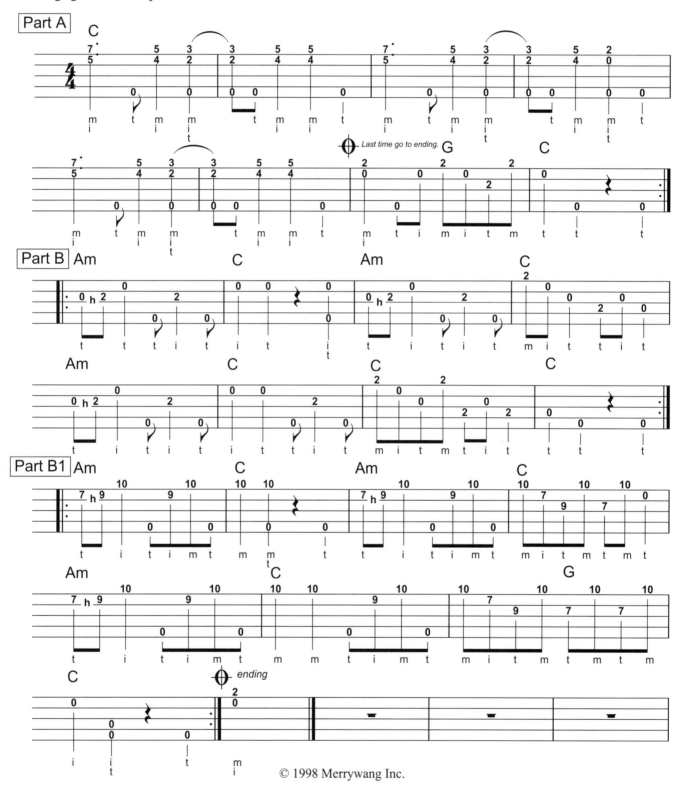

Mama Juana

Dudley Connell, Tony, Tom Gray, and Les Woodie, the players on
Sounds Like Bluegrass to Me. **Charlottesville, Virginia, 1999.**

Merrywang

"Merrywang's" triplets are simple once you figure them out: the right hand is thumb-finger-thumb, while the left hand does the pull-off immediately after the first thumb note is played. Also, on one A part I muffled the 5th string with the heel of my right hand's thumb for a more rhythmic sound. The guitar bass string is tuned from E down to D

Form: AA BB AA B1B1 AA BB AA

Composed by Tony Ellis

Tuning: gCGCD capo 2

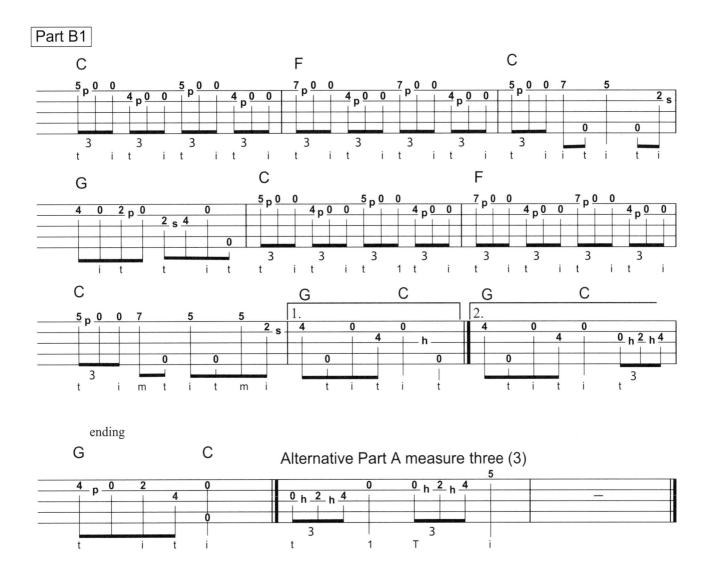

ending

Alternative Part A measure three (3)

51

Merrywang

Tony holding his gourd banjo at the 1996 Circleville, Ohio, Pumpkin Festival. In the 18th century, "merrywang" was a name reported for banjos of this design.

My Freedom Home

In "My Freedom Home," I tuned both the first and second strings to C, and then pitched
everything down to E on a nylon-strung fretless banjo. This two-finger style is one
I learned from James Jones, an old black man I knew as a child in Virginia. It is used
on many tunes I play for variation but entirely on this tune and the tune "Quaker Girl."
The right hand is basically thumb on 3rd, thumb on 5th, index on 1st, thumb on
3rd, followed by T-5, I-1, T-3, over and over in a loping manner.

Form: AA BB AA BB AA BB

Composed by Tony Ellis

Tuning: gCGCC (tuned down to bEBEE on recording)

My Freedom Home

My Mama Loves Me

"My Mama Loves Me" is to be played softly, inserting an E minor on the last time through for effect - a lullaby for my granddaughter Jenny.

Form: A B A1 B

Composed by Tony Ellis

Tuning: gCGCD   Capo 2

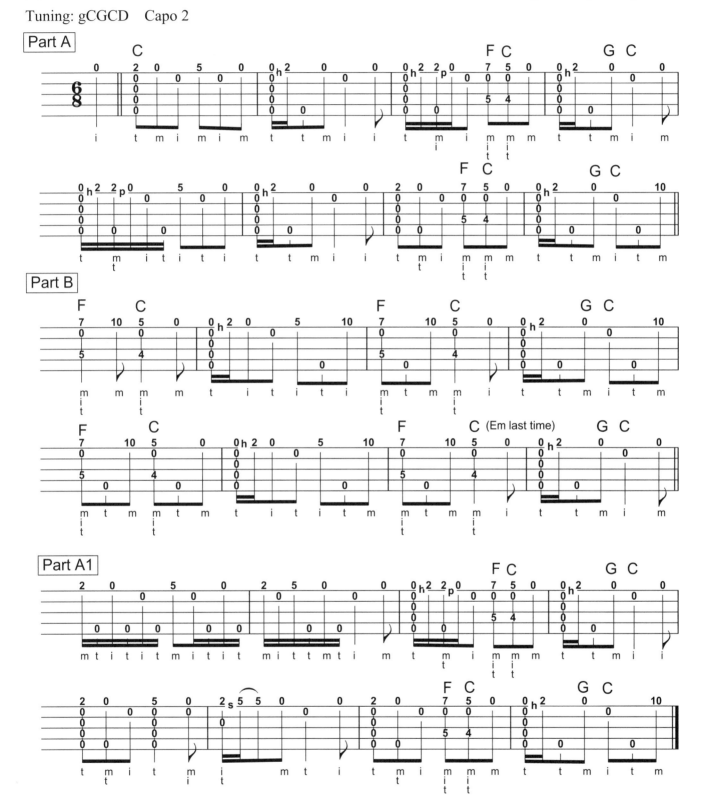

My Mama Loves Me

Tony at work on Sam Shepard's *A Lie of the Mind*, Lancaster, Pennsylvania, 1989.

Northwest Territory

At one point in "Northwest Territory," I gently muffle the fifth string on the B part
with the heel of the thumb of my right hand. This tune has sounds I recall from
Cherokee music. The guitar tuning is DADGAD capoed up 5 frets for effect.

Form: AA BB AA BB AA

Composed by Tony Ellis

Tuning: gDGCD

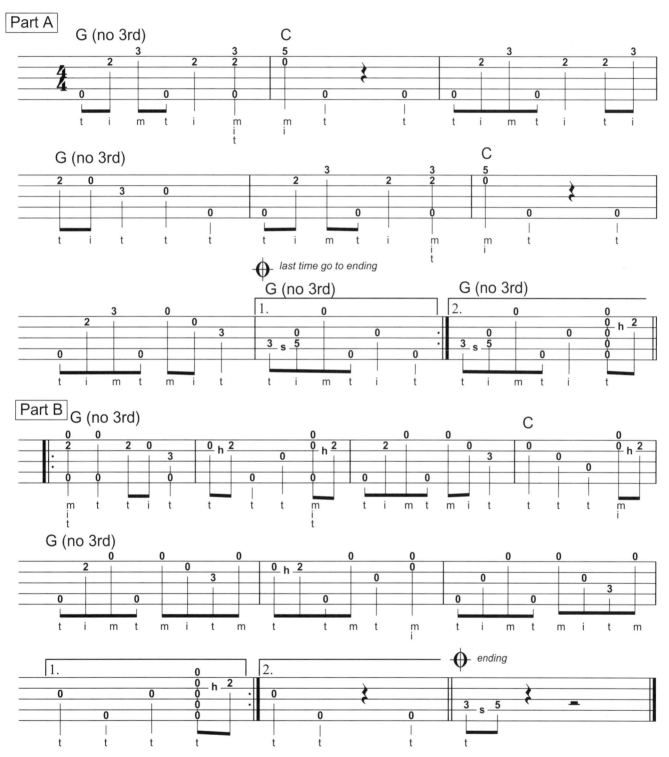

Northwest Territory

Swanson Walker and Tony, Peninsula, Ohio, 1983.
Swanson was Tony's first bluegrass banjo teacher.

Ohio Waltz

For the last two measures of "Ohio Waltz's" A part, the right hand index and middle
fingers move in to play the 3rd and 2nd strings. This adds nice harmonies to the bass
string. Waltzes provide a special opportunity for the banjo to express moods not normally
voiced -- romantic, melancholy, and gentle.

Form: AA B AA B AA B AA B

Composed by Tony Ellis

Tuning: gCGCD

Ohio Waltz

**Tony and the Musicians of Braeburn, Debbie Norris,
Gary Puckett, Lousie Adkins. Circleville, Ohio, 1996.**

Old Friends

Again, slow and gentle playing with a soft tone (away from the bridge) makes "Old Friends" most effective. To start, play a waltz timing pattern, 1,2,3 - 1,2,3 - 1,2,3 -1. Then begin the melody.

Tuning: gCGCD

Composed by Tony Ellis

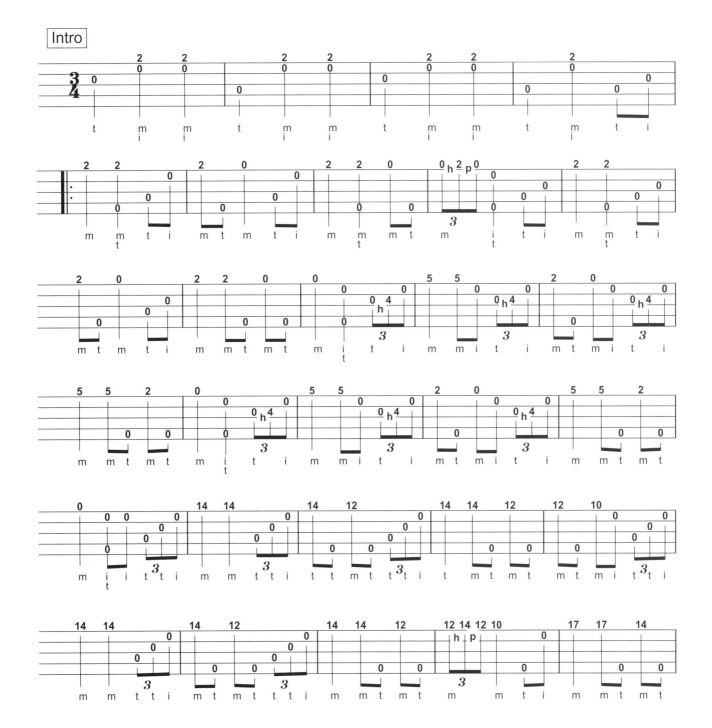

Old Friends

2

One-Horned Goat

"One-Horned Goat" begins with pull-offs and is easy to play. The tuning, eCGCD, is one
I learned from Fleming Brown's recording, *Little Rosewood Casket and Other Songs
of Joy* (which is still available on LP at my address for $10, which includes postage for
USA). Every banjo lover should have this album!

Form: AA BB CC AA BB CC AA BB CC

Composed by Tony Ellis

Tuning: eCGCD

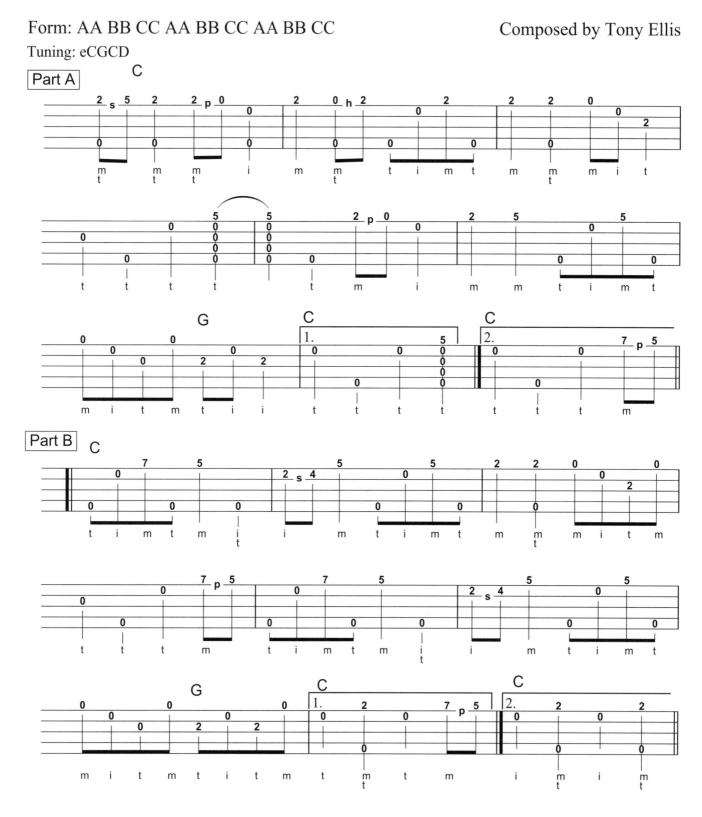

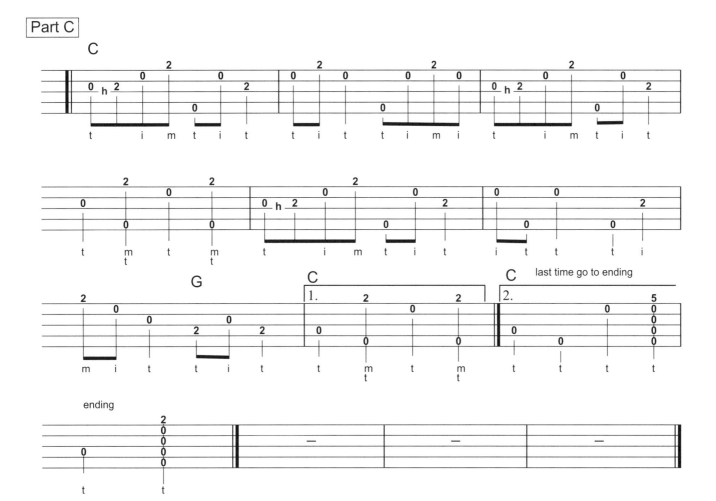

One-Horned Goat

Paint Creek

The banjo notes made with the left hand make "Paint Creek" sound as if the banjo were tuned in a modal tuning, but it is tuned at C/C. Growing up near the Cherokee reservation, I recall the feeling in Cherokee music and songs. The modal sounds in this tune reflect some of that. The guitar tuning is DGDGCD.

Form: AA BB AA BB AA BB AA

Composed by Tony Ellis

Tuning: gCGCD

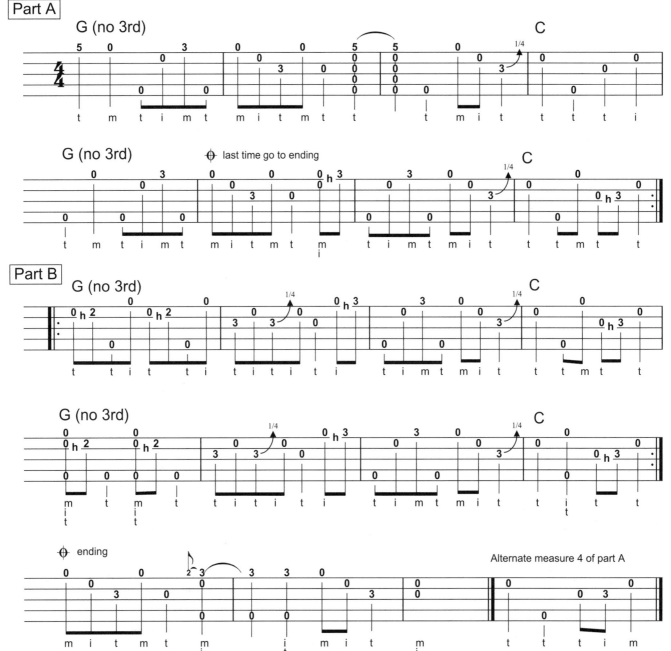

Paint Creek

John Jackson and Tony, 1995.

Peninsula

"Peninsula" is more like a bluegrass tune, peppy and fun! No really difficult notes,
but some notes could be made on strings other than specified. At times a note that
might be made on the 1st string should actually be made on the 2nd string due to
either physical distance to the next note or to make the right hand fingering fit better.
This is true of many situations in banjo playing and is something one develops in time
as a player.

Form: AA BB AA BB A1A1 B1B1 AA BB AA   Composed by Tony Ellis

Tuning: gCGCD capo 2

Peninsula

Tony at the 46th National Folk Festival, Peninsula, Ohio, 1984.

Pretty Little Waltz

"Pretty Little Waltz" uses mostly a two-finger approach with three fingers at times
to get underlying harmonies (open 2nd) while moving about with the melody and bass
string harmonies. It really is easy!

Form: A B A2 B A B

Composed by Tony Ellis

Tuning: gCGCD

last time to to ending

Part A2

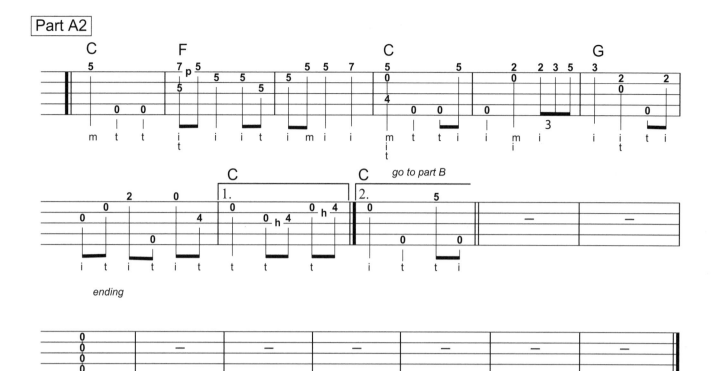

Pretty Little Waltz

Quaker Girl

"Quaker Girl" uses a standard G tuning lowered down to C on an old fretless banjo
with a simple two-finger technique T,T,F,T,F,T with the thumb playing the melody
notes the finger playing a filler note and then the thumb playing a timing note on the 5th
string. Example T 3rd, T 5th, F 1st, T 3rd / T5th, F 1st, T 3rd / T 5th, F 1st, T 5th / and
so on in a loping manner.

Form: AA B A1A1 B AA B A

Composed by Tony Ellis

Tuning: gDGBD (Tuned to cGCEG on recording)

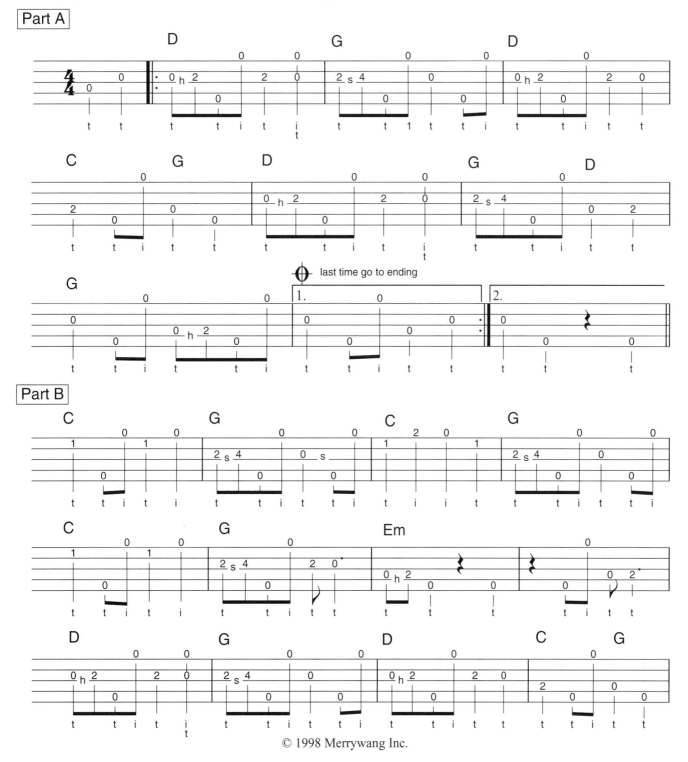

© 1998 Merrywang Inc.

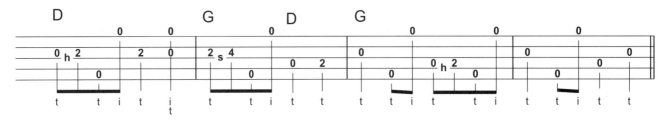

Part A1

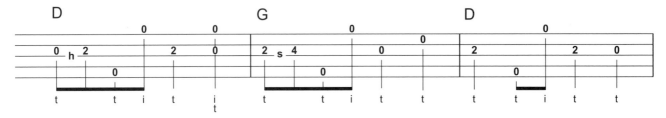

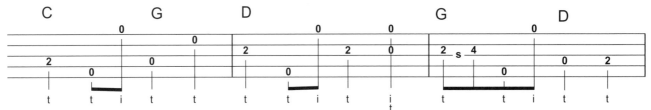

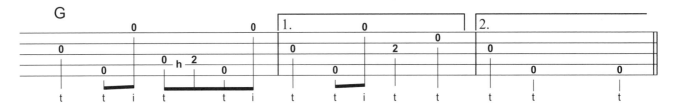

ending

74

Quaker Girl

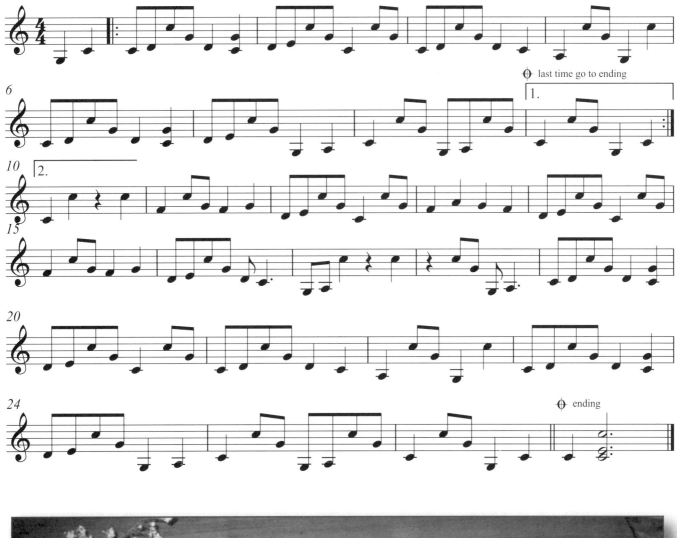

Fretless banjo used on "Quaker Girl"

Rain on the Water

The A part of "Rain on the Water" is two-finger style and the B part is three-finger style.
The two-finger part is a rhythmic sounding movement and is a close cousin to frailing
in the evolution of banjo styles. The right hand finger and thumb would play F, F, T, F,
T, F, T, F, etc.

Form: A BB A BB A BB

Composed by Tony Ellis

Tuning: gCGCD

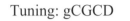

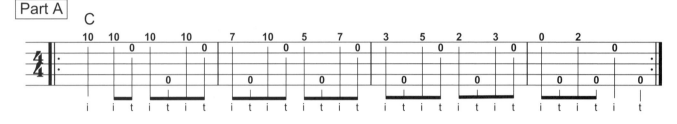

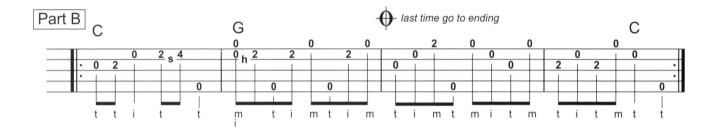

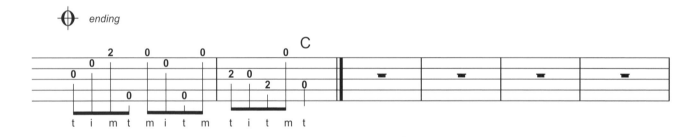

Rain on the Water

"Dr. Mongle's Old-Time Music Machine," Dr. Bruce Mongle, Little Joe Mongle, Tony, Jim Bullock, Frank Buchanan, and Hump Doyle. Bristol, Tennessee, 1972.

Red Dog

Though played in F tuning, "Red Dog's" three-finger and two-finger approach is similar to the simple loping two-finger style in "Quaker Girl." This is a tune that has brought together elements of bluegrass and old-time. It also mimics a dog barking!

Form: AA BB AA BB AA BB AA

Tuning: fCFCD

Composed by Tony Ellis

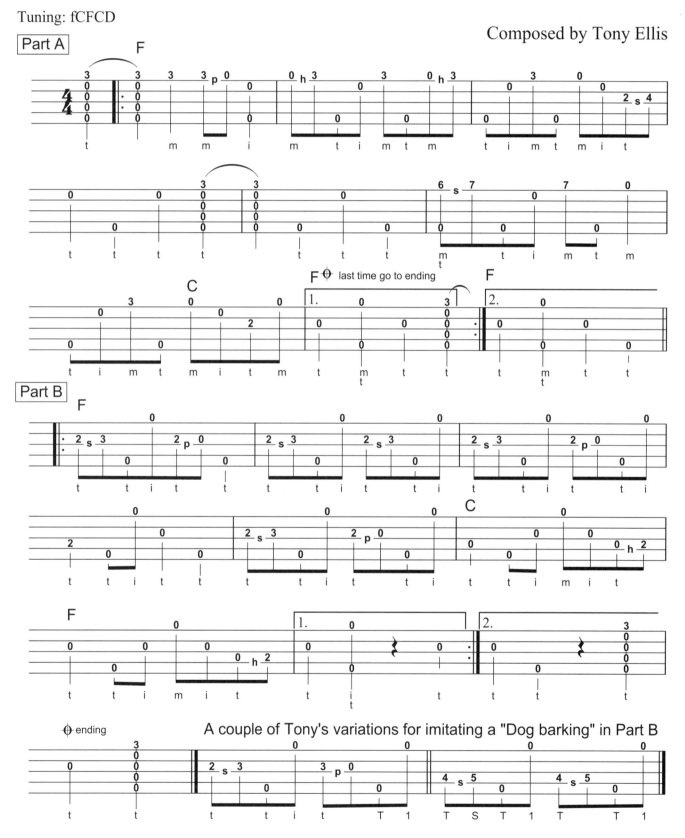

A couple of Tony's variations for imitating a "Dog barking" in Part B

Red Dog

Seleshe Damessae and Tony at the 1996 National Folk Festival.
Seleshe's *krar*, an ancient Ethiopian lute, bears a banjo-like sound.

Rocky Road to Kansas

In "Rocky Road to Kansas," when playing the bass part (part B) the right hand index and middle fingers cover one string and play the 3rd and 2nd strings as counterpoint to the melody line. This tune projects a mood as much as a melody.

Form: AA BB AA B1B1 AA BB AA B1B1

Composed by Tony Ellis

Tuning: gCGCD capo 2

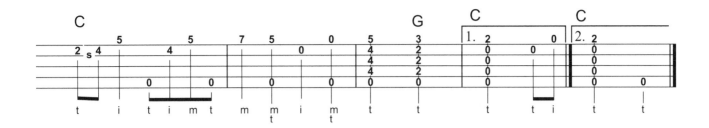

Rocky Road to Kansas

Sally Ann

When playing "Sally Ann" in the lower register (bass string notes), bring the right hand
fingers over one string to play the 3rd and 2nd strings while the thumb plays the melody.

Form: AA B CC DD A1A1 B

Traditional, arranged by Tony Ellis

Tuning: gCGCD capo 2

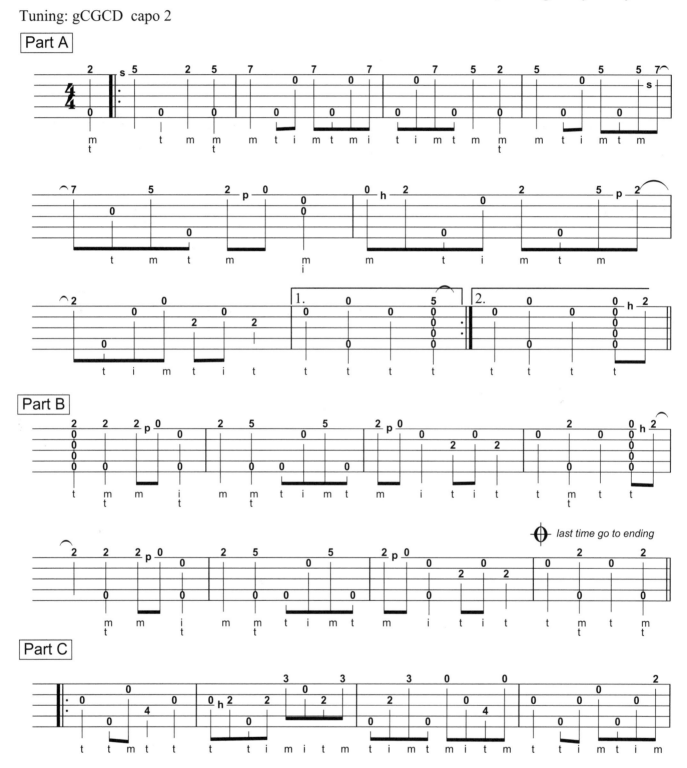

last time go to ending

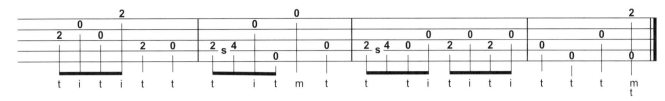

Part D

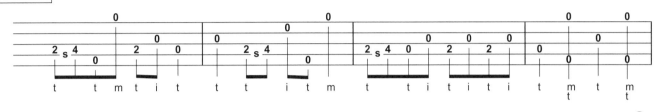

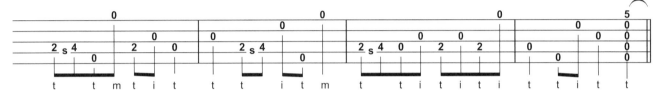

Part A1

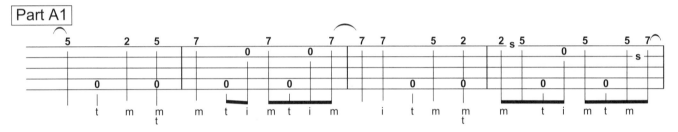

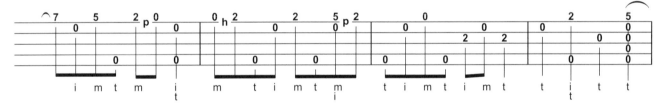

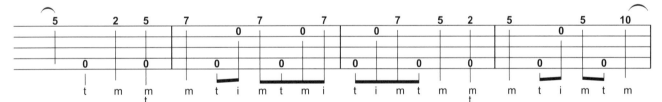

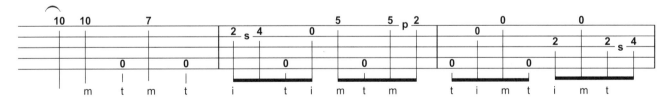

ending

Sally Ann

Shortenin' Bread

"Shortenin' Bread" is a straight ahead bluegrass version. The last roll on each line is
the same roll one might use as the first roll on "Cumberland Gap." Learn the tune first
at a moderate speed; then you can easily play it fast.

Form: A B A B1 (fiddle) A B A1 B1 Tag   Traditional, arranged by Tony Ellis

Tuning: gDGBD   Capo 2

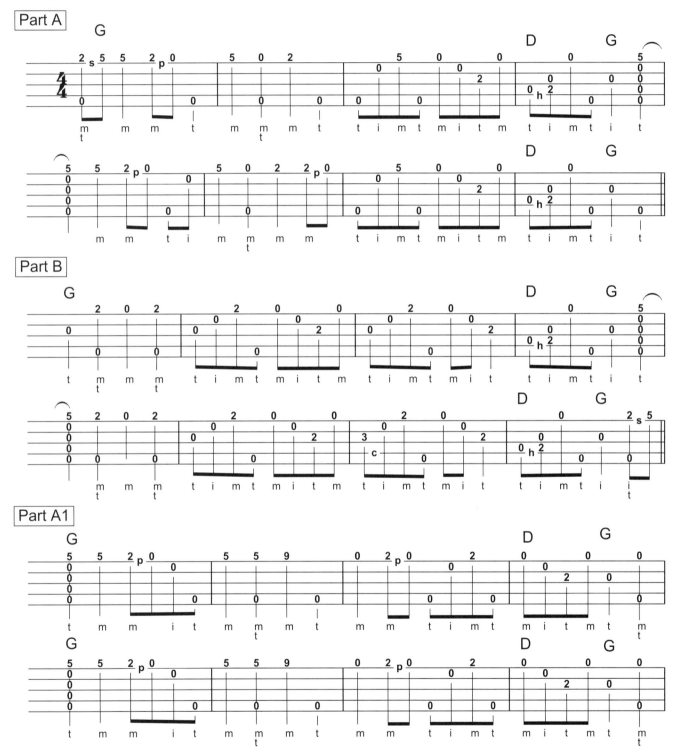

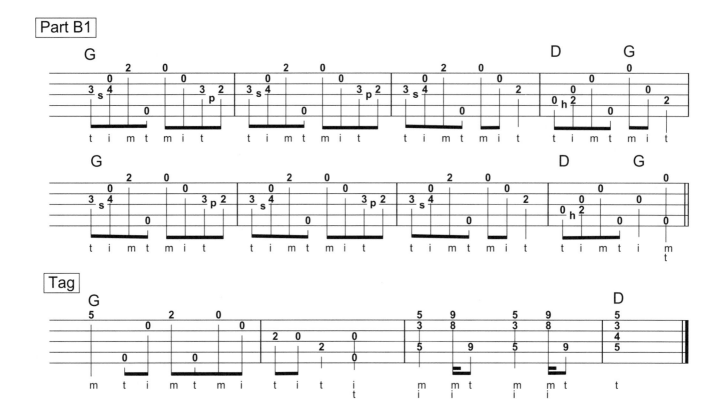

Shortenin' Bread

Silver Dollar

While "Silver Dollar' employs mostly three-finger style, the B part is at times done with the loping two-finger method (see "Quaker Girl"), giving this tune an old feel. The third part musically simulates the ringing sound of a silver dollar being flipped into the air!

Form: AA BB CC AA B1B1 CC AA BB CC AA

Composed by Tony Ellis

Tuning: gCGCD

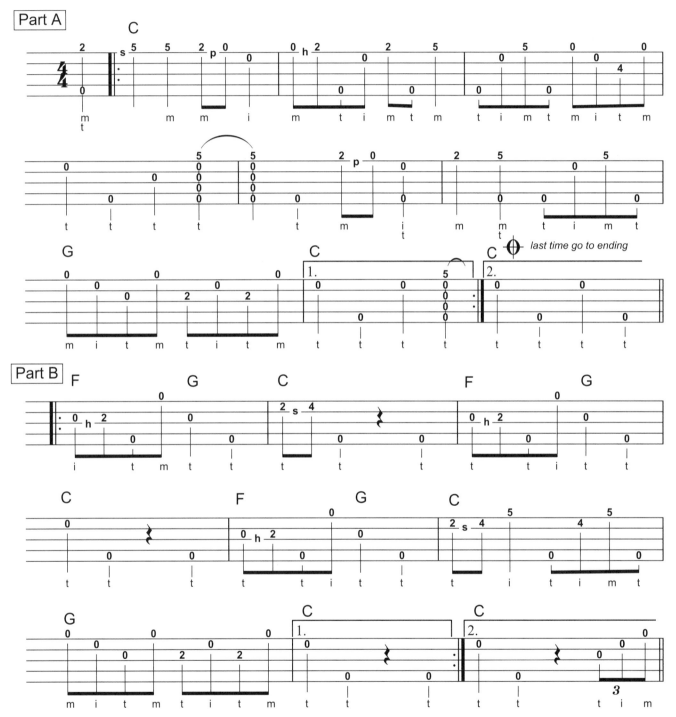

Silver Dollar

last time go to ending

ending

Fiddler Les Woodie and Tony, Charlottesville, Virginia, 1999.

Snow Camp

"Snow Camp's" tuning comes from my hearing Stephen Wade play Hobart Smith's "Last Chance." There are variations to this tuning which have special effects on some tunes, i.e., the bass string tuned to D rather than C. This tune falls into place easily and the twelve-string guitar accompaniment adds a lot to this tune.

Form: AA BB AA BB A1A1 BB AA

Composed by Tony Ellis

Tuning: fCFCD

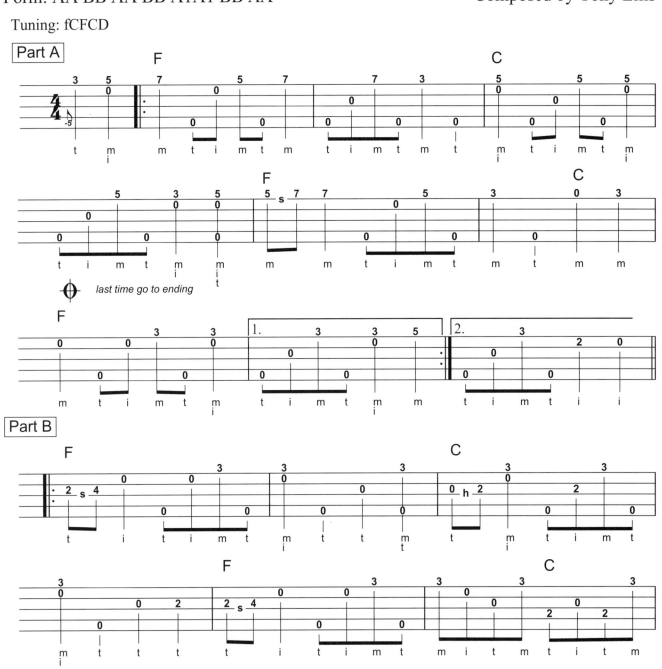

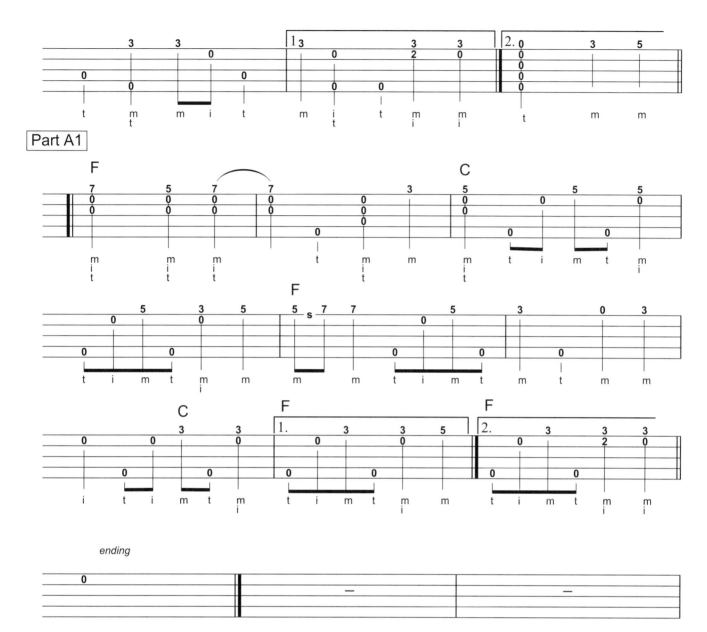

Part A1

ending

Snow Camp

last time go to ending

ending

Stephen

"Stephen" can be played in C or D as easily as E♭ (its setting on *Dixie Banner*). This should be played at a slow to moderate tempo. The high note ending to the B part is a little strange at first but is syncopated and will fall into place after a bit!

Form: AA B AA B1 AA B AA

Composed by Tony Ellis

Tuning: gCGCD   capo 3

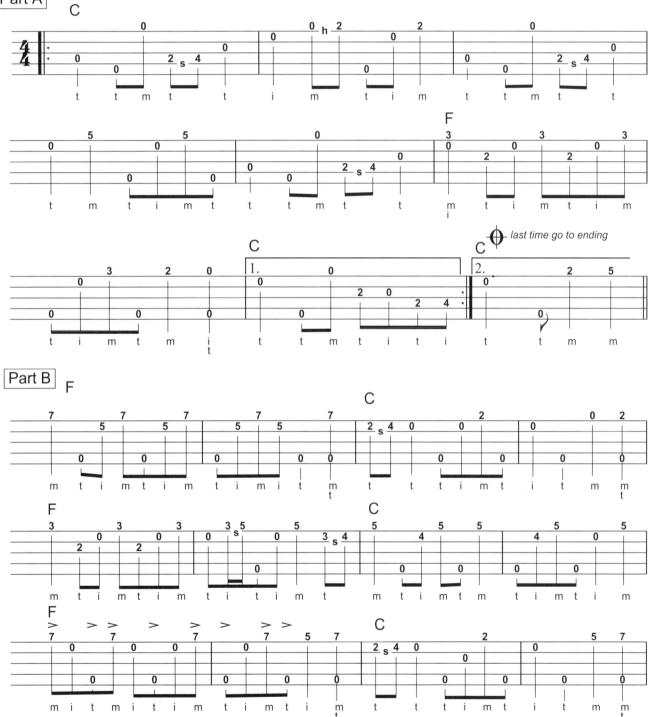

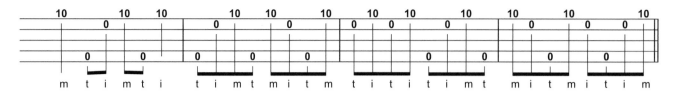

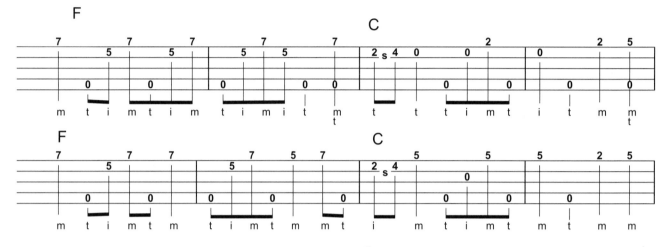

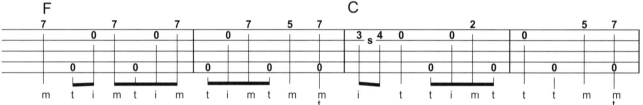

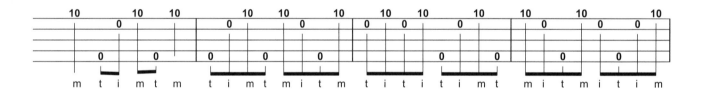

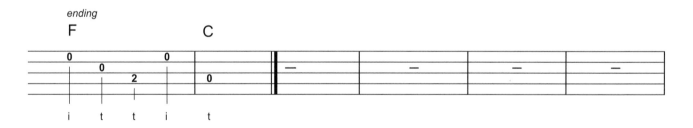

ending

94

Stephen

last time go to ending

1.

2.

ending

Straw Dolls

"Straw Dolls" should be played gently and away from the bridge to create a softer and warmer tone. This tune was inspired by a five year old Japanese child who wanted to show me her homemade, straw-filled doll.

Form: A B A1 B A

Composed by Tony Ellis

Tuning: gCGCD

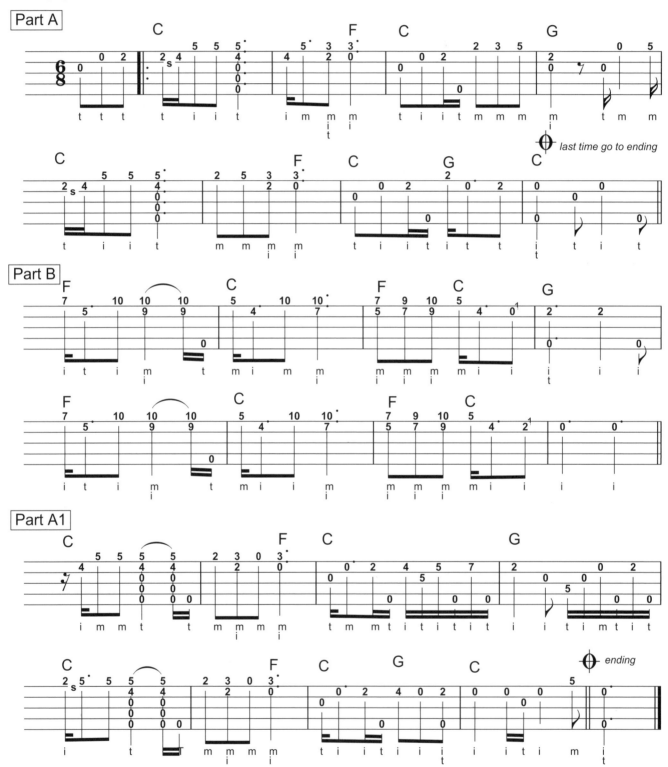

Straw Dolls

Tony, Charlottesville, Virginia, 1999

T-Model Ford

"T-Model Ford" is mostly three-finger but also uses two-finger style at one point on the A part. I can remember riding in these contraptions many times and how fun they were: rough riding, gears grinding, roaring mechanical marvels!

Form: AA BB A1A1 B1 AA BB AA

Composed by Tony Ellis

Tuning: gCGCD

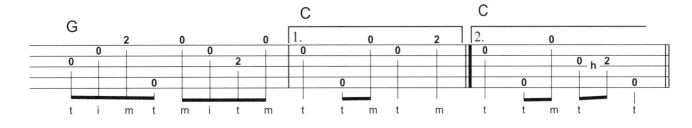

Part A1

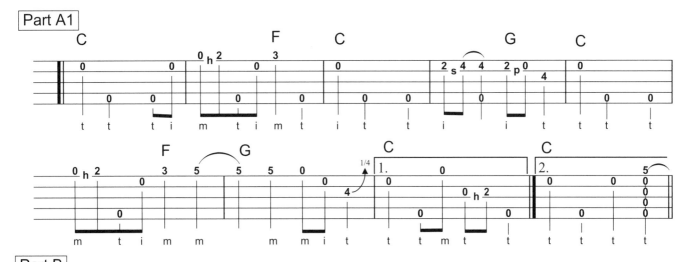

Part B

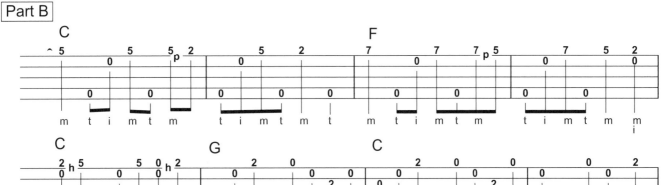

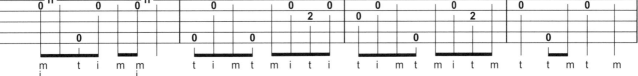

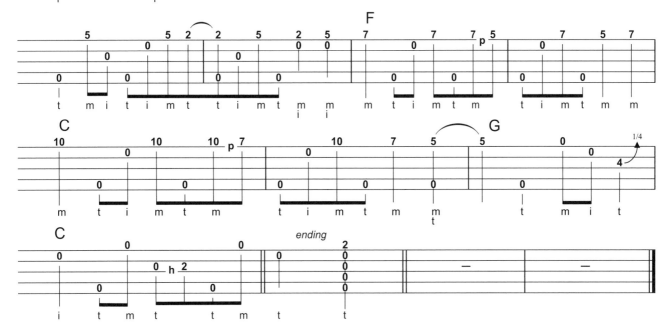

The Hangman's Song

At on point on the B part (third time through) of "The Hangman's Song," I muffle the 5th string with the heel of the thumb of my right hand for a rhythmic sound resembling the slow gallop of a horse taking the hangman to his next job.

Form: AA BB Vrs 1 AA BB Vrs 2 AA BB Vrs 1 AA

Composed by Tony Ellis

Tuning: gDGCD

Hangman, hangman hang 'em up high. Watch 'em kick and watch 'em die.
Hangman, hangman do your little dance, for the devil's gonna get you one morning.
Oil them ropes and tie them knots, stand 'em in a line.
Pull the handle with a yank, six hanging at a time.

The Hangman's Song

Johnny Palmer, Don Reno, Tony, Red Smiley, and Mack Magaha, Roanoke, Virginia, 1958.

Trail of Tears

To play "Trail of Tears," manually capo at the 2nd fret with the left index finger. The 5th string should be raised to A. This tune reflects the anguish of the forced march of the Cherokee from North Carolina to Oklahoma -- a sad chapter in American history.

Tuning: aCGCD

Composed by Tony Ellis

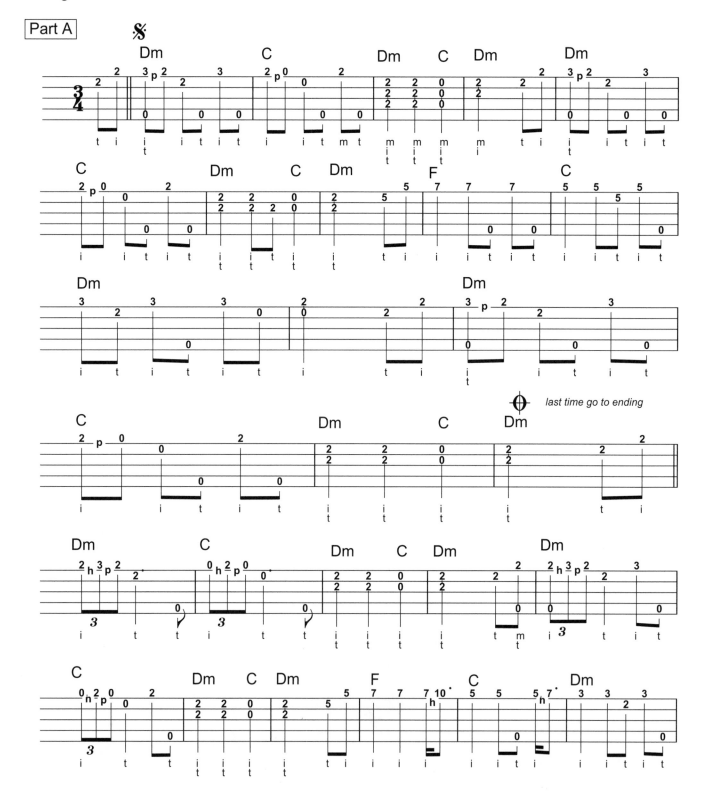

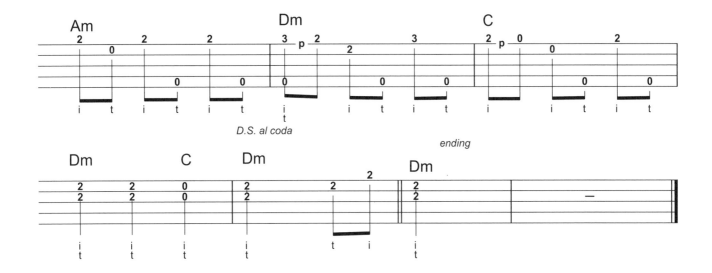

D.S. al coda

ending

Trail of Tears

Uncle Shorty

"Uncle Shorty" is best played at a moderate speed -- not so fast! Try to think about a lovable old character who has been in the pub a bit too long, as he does a little soft-shoe for his pals.

Form: AA BB AA BB AA B1B1

Composed by Tony Ellis

Tuning: gCGCD

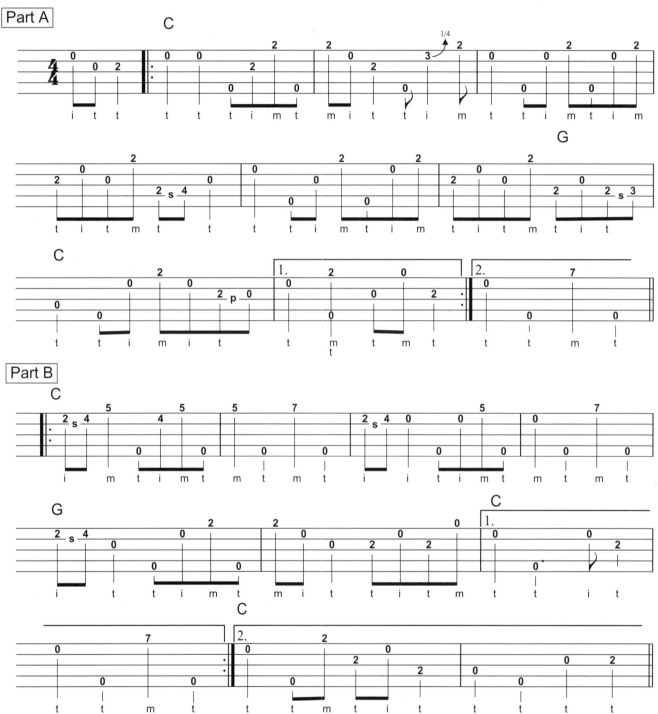

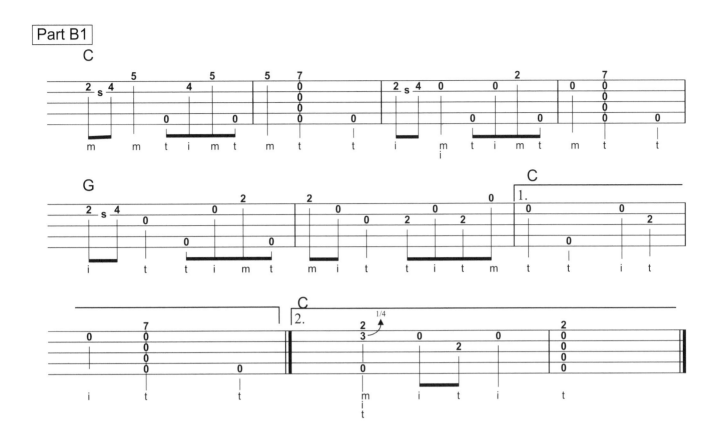

Uncle Shorty

last time go to ending

Wade's Dixieliner Special Railroad Blues # 9

When playing the A part of "Wade's Dixieliner Special Railroad Blues #9," hold down the left index finger on the 2nd string, 1st fret to give a 'modal' sound. On the B part the 2nd string must be at the normal note of B when open. Sort of typical bluegrass picking -- up tempo with a lot of movement and drive.

Form: AA B AA B AA

Composed by Tony Ellis

Tuning: gDGBD

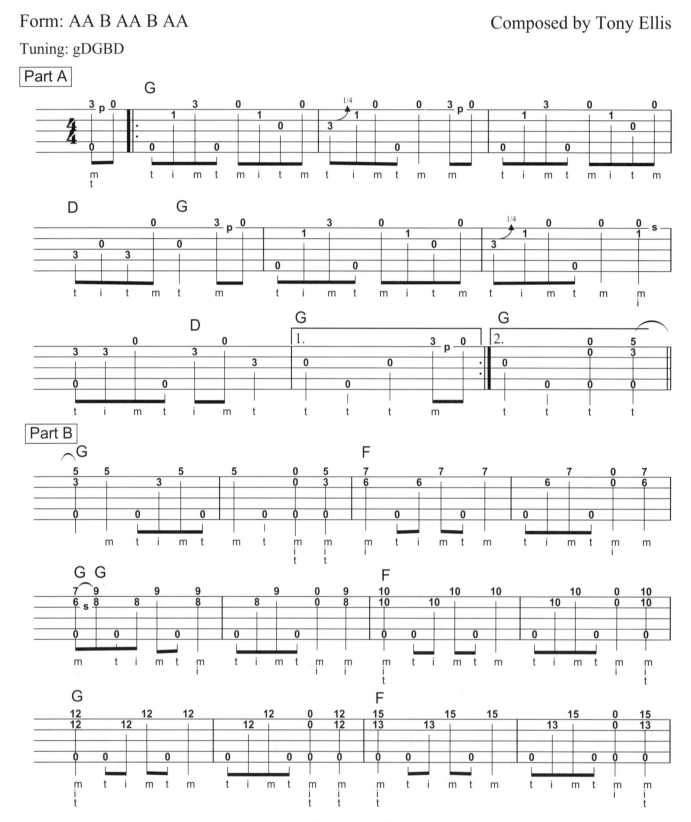

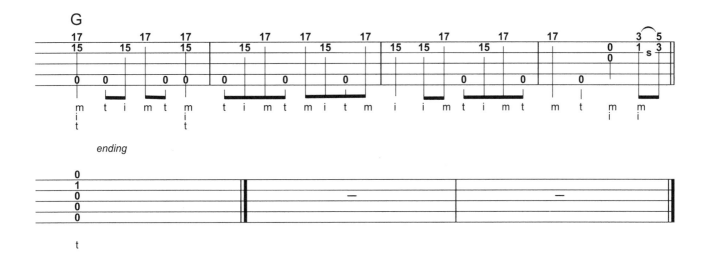

Wade's Dixieliner Special Railroad Blues #9

West Virginia Joe

"West Virginia Joe" should present no big problems. It's pretty straight ahead bluegrass picking with a sprightly tempo and standard bluegrass rolls. It even has an E minor!!!

Form: AA BB AA BB AA BB

Composed by Tony Ellis

Tuning: gDGBD

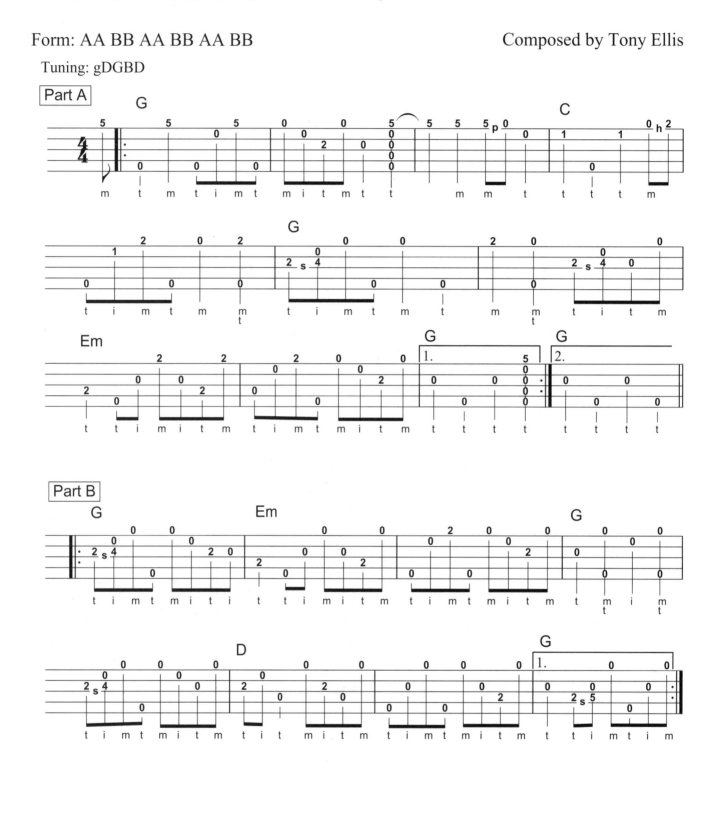

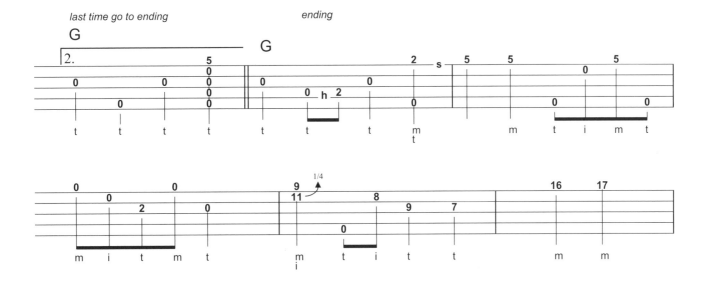

Alternate Part A measure 2 played after first time through part A.

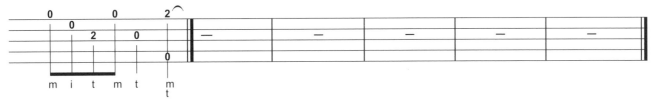

West Virginia Joe

last time go to ending

ending

109

When I Think of You

"When I Think of You" is to be played slowly and gently. At the place where you slow down (after having come down the neck), take a deep breath while the notes are allowed to fade! This tune was recorded with a Celtic harp (to represent a female voice) and banjo (the male voice).

Tuning: gCGCD

Composed by Tony Ellis

When I Think of You

Bessie Lee Maudlin, Bill Monroe, Carter Stanley, Bobby Smith, and Tony Ellis. Mt. Jackson, Virginia, 1961.

Wild Fox

Even with its fast pace, play the A part of "Wild Fox" pretty softly, and then add power on the B part. The simple two-finger A part represents the fox hiding for a moment, catching his breath, and the B part explodes as the fox goes tearing off again! Don't play this at a rest home unless you have liability insurance!

Form: AA BB AA BB A1A1 BB AA BB A1A1 BB AA   Composed by Tony Ellis

Tuning: gCGCD

© 1993 Merrywang Inc.

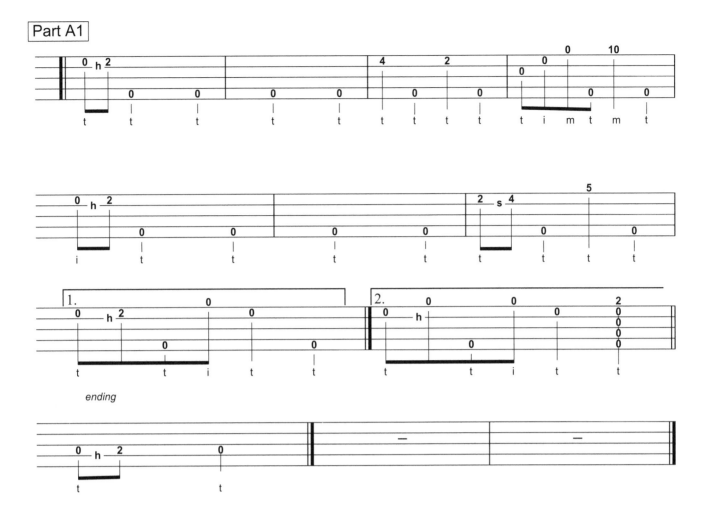

Wild Fox

113

Wind Chimes and Nursery Rhymes

The slow and gentle "Wind Chimes and Nursery Rhymes" is a lullaby using the first
string as the main melody vehicle. The third string is used a lot for harmony--a technique
I first learned from my early banjo hero, teacher, mentor, and friend, Don Reno. At the point
near the end of the tune when the notes are slowed and faded, take a deep breath to
make sure the fade is effective.

Form: AA B AA B

Composed by Tony Ellis

Tuning: gCGCD

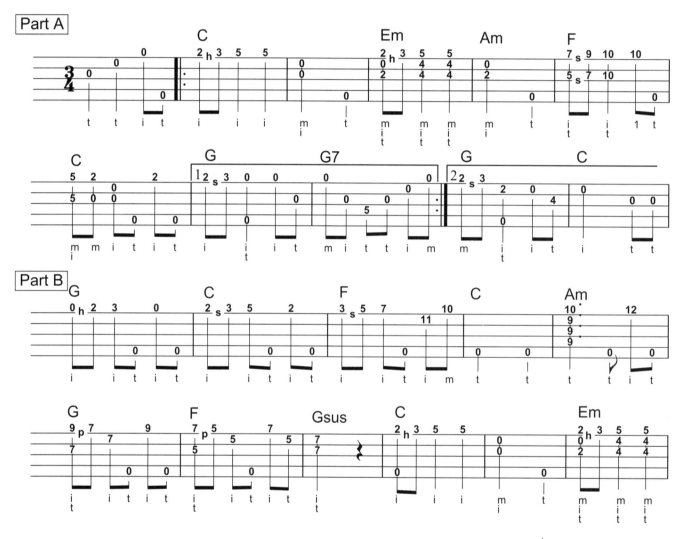

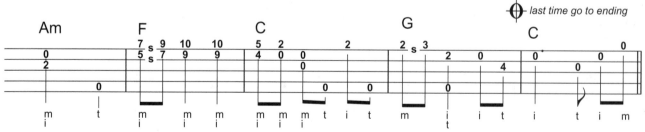

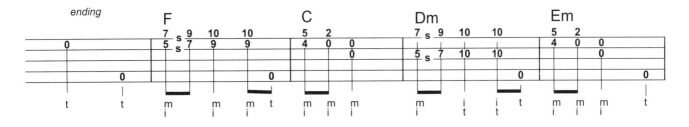

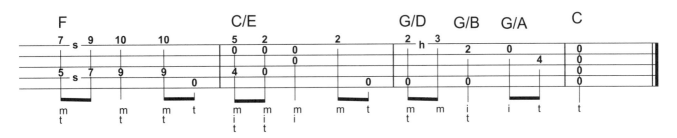

Wind Chimes and Nursery Rhymes

Charlie Ellis, Tony's grandfather, Siler City, North Carolina, 1910.

Tony Ellis on LP and CD

Mr Bluegrass. Bill Monroe and His Blue Grass Boys. Decca DL4080. 1961

Bluegrass Ramble. Bill Monroe and His Blue Grass Boys. Decca DL74266. 1962

Bluegrass Special. Bill Monroe and His Blue Grass Boys. Decca DL4387. 1962

I'll Meet You in Church Sunday Morning. Bill Monroe and His Blue Grass Boys. Decca DL4537. 1964

Walkin' in Big Tracks. Wiley Smith. Gotta Go Records. 1972

Seems Like Romance to Me. Various artists. Gambier Folklore Society GFS 901. 1985

Righteous Blues. Bill Ellis. Marimac 8003. 1987.

Farmer's Frolic. Ross County Farmers. Marimac 9013. 1987

Dixie Banner. Tony Ellis. Flying Fish FF444. 1987

Bluegrass 1959-1969. Bill Monroe. Bear Family Records BCD 15529-4 DH. 1991

Freedoms Reborn. Various artists. Scioto Valley Arts Council. 1992.

Highland Soul. Zan McLeod. Joy of Music JMCD001. 1993.

Farewell My Home. Tony Ellis. Flying Fish FF70620. 1993.

Masters of the Banjo. Various artists. Arhoolie CD421. 1994.

Dancing in the Parlor. Stephen Wade. County Records CO-CD-2721. 1997

The Art of the Banjo. Various artists. Sonoton SCB 248. 1997.

Gaelic Roots. Various artists. Kells KM9514. 1997.

Quaker Girl. Tony Ellis. County CO-CD-2723. 1998.

Rich at the Roots. Various artists. North American Folk Alliance FA002. 1998.

The Full Catastrophe. Bill Ellis. Bell Weather Records 497. 1999.

Sounds Like Bluegrass to Me. Tony Ellis. Copper Creek CC0174. 1999.

Good Ole Corn! David Verny Band. Roundtown Records 019. 2000.

American Traveler. Bill Monroe. County Records CCS-119. 2000.

I'll Just Steal Away and Pray. Various artists. Copper Creek CCCD-0197. 2001.

Living in the Name of Love. Various artists. Copper Creek CCCD-0198. 2001.

Gold Rush at Copper Creek. Various artists. Copper Creek CCCD-6001. 2002.

Conqueroo. William Lee Ellis. Yellow Dog Records YDR 1043. 2002.

Horatio's Drive. Various artists. Columbia Records CK90659. 2003.

Film, TV, and Video

Wild California. Sea Studios. 1989.

Echoes of America. Principal Film Company. 1990.

The Cuyahoga: Portrait of a Crooked River. Kent State University. 1994.

Baseball. Ken Burns. Florentine Films. 1994.

Banjo Bash at Buckeystown. Maryland Banjo Academy. 1998.

Party of Five. Fox Network. 1999.

Tony Ellis, Banjo Old and New. Cedar Glade Productions 006. 1999.

America's Voices: Celebrating Life. Travel Channel. 2003.

Horatio's Drive. Ken Burns. Florentine Films. 2003.

Pictured on the back cover are *Dixie Banner*, Flying Fish FF 70444; *Farewell My Home*, Flying Fish FF 70620; *Quaker Girl*, County CO-CD-2723; and *Sounds Like Bluegrass to Me*, Copper Creek CCCD-0174. Tony also appears on *Masters of the Banjo*, Arhoolie CD421. These recordings provide the tunes that comprise this book.